R. H. Schively

Holy-Day Stories

Christmas, Good Friday, Easter Ascension, Whitsuntide

R. H. Schively

Holy-Day Stories
Christmas, Good Friday, Easter Ascension, Whitsuntide

ISBN/EAN: 9783743419773

Manufactured in Europe, USA, Canada, Australia, Japa

Cover: Foto ©Lupo / pixelio.de

Manufactured and distributed by brebook publishing software (www.brebook.com)

R. H. Schively

Holy-Day Stories

Holy-Day Stories:

CHRISTMAS,   GOOD FRIDAY,

EASTER,

ASCENSION,   WHITSUNTIDE.

———o———

TRANSLATED BY

R. H. SCHIVELY.

———o———

PHILADELPHIA:
Reformed Church Publication Board,
54 NORTH SIXTH STREET.

THIS BOOK
IS PUBLISHED BY THE
Fund of the Zion Sunday-School
OF THE
Ref. Church, Chambersburg, Pa.

Entered, according to Act of Congress in the year 1869, by
REFORMED CHURCH PUBLICATION BOARD,
In the Clerk's Office of the District Court, for the Eastern District of Pennsylvania.

JAS. B. RODGERS CO.,
ELECTROTYPERS AND PRINTERS,
52 & 54 N. Sixth St.

Christmas.

CHRISTMAS EVE IN THE WOODS.

I DO not doubt, my dear children, that you all agree with me, that no day in all the year is more welcome than the one on which we say "This is Christmas Eve!" You, who live in the towns, tell me if the first glance from the window on that morning, is not most delightful? Do not all the houses in the long rows stand in a pleasant, mysterious quiet? Within each window, is a joyful expectation of Christmas. Behind each closed door some wonderful secret preparation is in progress.

Where our eyes can discover nothing, there imagination is most busy; and in all things which usually pass quite unnoticed, children's bright, curious gaze is sure, to-day, to discover some great mystery. If the good God has clothed the earth in a white winter garment, it seems to us on that morning, purer and fairer than usual; and if the glorious sunshine scatters its thousands of pearls and diamonds upon it, then, indeed, it shines as clear and brilliant as the light of joy which the anticipation of Christmas calls up in your young hearts. At home, nothing but secrets. Here a mysterious room; there a significantly closed cupboard. Turn your eyes out of doors, children; pass away the time until the pleasant evening hour, by looking out of the windows.

Indeed, much may be seen outside; for outside is the whole world, and in the whole world to-day is Christmas Eve.

With what busy haste every one in the street goes in and out, backward and forward. Is there not something peculiar in the very sound of the doors as they quickly open and close, and of the rapid footsteps that enter and depart from them? Do not all faces glow with unusual eagerness; a smile full of hope and of promise? Ah! happy children, you read everywhere to-day, "This is Christmas Eve."

Perhaps the thought has scarcely ever occurred to you that there are children in the world to whom this day brings no pleasure; for in your joyous imagination you light up a Christmas tree for every one, and fancy your own happiness poured into all hearts. Know, then, that Christmas brings sorrow, as well as joy; hear a tale of Christmas Eve—beautiful, yet mournful.

Ah, it is true, that not all enjoy this blessed season! Many, many children there are, for whom no Christmas tree is ever lighted; and many for whose eyes its beauties shine, while to their hearts it brings no pleasure. I will tell you first of these, that you may realize, if you can, the sad truth that there are children without childlike pleasures, and brilliant Christmas trees, by which no heart grows warm.

Leopold and Elmina, like most young people on Christmas Eve, stood looking out of the windows. They were the children of a wealthy and distinguished citizen; some counsellor, perhaps, whose stately house, like its owner, bore itself proudly among its more humble neighbors. Leopold and Elmina were, indeed, waiting for the evening. But the hours seemed long and tedious to them; for the holy significance of the Christmas festival had no power over their hearts, and they took little pleasure even in their fine gifts, because they could enjoy such things every day.

At such Christmas gatherings, in so many wealthy families, it seems to be the only concern of those who call themselves the *friends* of the children, to vie with each other in overloading them with fashionable, but useless articles; which gifts, on the succeeding days, are always criticized and compared with scrutinizing eyes. In compliance with this custom the counsellor never failed at Christmas to fill a large room for his children with costly gifts, which in the evening were illuminated with a flood of light. Yet these rich children were probably, of all in the city, the poorest in happiness; they thought the old custom of the evening surprise an extremely disagreeable one, for how *should* they pass the long hours of the day?

They had eaten Christmas cakes all the morning, in consequence of which they were uncomfortable and quite out of humor. For half an hour, now, Leopold had found no amusement, save that of making faces at every passer-by who happened to glance at the lofty dwelling, while Elmina devoted herself to the cruel pastime of plucking a feather every few moments from a poor screaming parrot. Suddenly the boy cried out:

"Oh, look at these dirty little creatures; how saucily they peep in here, without being at all ashamed of their rags. Indeed, I do believe they want to come in."

This diverted Elmina's attention from the tormented bird, to the poor children in the street. It was a brother and sister, Anthony and Marietta; who, in old, worn-out clothing, wandered along shivering with cold—two of those destitute little ones who have no Christmas tree lighted up for them.

"Listen, they are coming in," said Leopold. "I heard the door-bell ring; that will be a Christmas show such as we never had here before."

The two timid children were indeed already standing in the magnificent entrance hall; they had come in to sing a Christmas carol, but before their poor white lips could commence the song, something happened to fill their childish hearts with grief.

"A very rich lord must live here, don't you think so?" softly asked the little girl of her brother, who was somewhat older than she; "see how beautiful everything is; they will surely have a little gift to spare us. O Anthony," she cried, with sudden delight, "look, here is a door open; what elegant things are in that room! What a Christmas Eve! that grand tree with all those candles; if we could only see them lighted!" And so saying, she drew her brother involuntarily to the half-open door of the large parlor, where the gifts of Leopold and Elmina were prepared for the evening surprise.

The children could not resist the temptation to step in, and the brilliant sight held them spell-bound. Marietta had almost devoutly folded her hands, while Anthony humbly removed his cap; then, after looking at the grand display for a few moments with eager, sparkling eyes, the little sister drew a long sigh of admiration, and said:

"Ah, brother, some children whom Christ loves very much, must live in this house!"

But their admiration was suddenly interrupted by a movement at the door, and a harsh voice behind them calling out, "Catch the little thieves!"

The children uttered a cry of terror, and darted out into the hall, where they found themselves surrounded by all the servants, who had hurried up at the alarm. The counsellor himself ran out of his room, and called out angrily to the children:

"What are you doing here? What mischief have you done? What wickedness led you into that room?"

Marietta could not speak for crying, but Anthony said humbly:

"We beg pardon, good sir; we came in because we were hungry, and we hoped for a little Christmas gift, and we went into that room," he added, hesitating, as the memory of the words "You little thieves" called a deep flush to his cheeks, "we went into that room, good sir, to see the beautiful things; but indeed, indeed, not to take them." "Ah," he said, in a low, devout tone, "could we so grieve the holy Saviour to-day, who made us so happy last Christmas?"

"Enough, enough, you shameless little rascal," snarled the counsellor; "you saucy beggars are all alike; one must be careful to keep you outside of his doors. The poor-taxes are heavy enough now-a-days for a man to enjoy at least a little peace in his house."

So saying, the rich man turned his back on the poor children. Anthony and Marietta moved toward the door, but behind them sprang out a bad boy; it was Leopold, who, with his sister, had watched for their going out, armed with his whip, that he might amuse himself by chasing the poor children with it. But the blow he aimed at them did not reach them. A compassionate servant quickly closed the door behind them. The rich children laughed mockingly, and the poor ones again stood outside. Alone, outside in the cold, cold world, in which to-day was Christmas Eve.

"Anthony," said Marietta, in a low voice, "let us not go among rich people again to-day. I do not believe the holy Saviour lives where they have so many fine things."

* * * * * *

"Could we so grieve the holy Saviour to-day, who made us so happy last Christmas?"

These were the words the rich man had heard with unmoved heart; yet in them was contained all the history of these poor children. Yes, on the last Christmas, they had had, though not a grand tree, yet still a little one, beautiful to them, for a mother's tender love had lighted it up. Frau Magdalene had added so many nights to her days of ceaseless labor, that she had earned a few shillings to spend on a Christmas treat for her children. And how happy she was when she had lighted up the little tree with its three candles, laying under it a warm garment and a gay pictured Bible for each, with a few spice-nuts. But this was Frau Magdalene's last indulgence. On that very Christmas Eve, while singing with her children the Hymn to the Saviour, she felt an irresistible longing, as though her spirit were drawn heavenward. Only a few weeks from that time, she was laid in the grave, and Anthony and Marietta were alone in the world.

They were taken from their own home and sent to board with a man who asked but little for taking care of them, because he did less—that is, nothing, for them; for at night they slept in a cold, dark room, and during the day he sent them out to beg. It was, indeed, a wicked, drunken man, to whose care the unfortunate little orphans had been intrusted. Even on this Christmas Eve they were obliged to wander in the cold streets, while he drank and gambled at the tavern.

Whither should they go now? "Little

thieves!" seemed to ring in their ears, whenever they approached a house-door, and, timid and fearful, they turned away.

"Come, little sister," said Anthony at last; "do not look so sad. It is Christmas Eve everywhere in the world to-day, and not only where rich people live; it is Christmas Eve for us too."

Further and further, they went silently on, till at last the little girl asked:

"What do you think, Anthony; which way shall we go?"

"Out of the town, I think," answered the brother; "it will soon be evening, and then it will be bright enough in the houses, but dark in the streets, and darker still in our cold room. Outside of town we shall have the broad sky, full of starlight, and a road through the woods leads to the farm where the good countryman lives who used sometimes to send mother some soup, when she was sick; perhaps he will give us a warm little corner to sleep in to-night."

So the children passed out of town. Little Marietta looked back now and then, for she fancied that she already saw lights burning here and there, the bright Christmas candles. But Anthony never turned; he only sought the road that led into the woods, and there before him it lay, white and glittering, under a hard frozen snow. The twilight now began to be cheered by the light of the stars, only a few, at first, coming softly into view; but directly they sparkled brightly forth, quickly lighting up all the sky.

"See, there are our Christmas lights," said the brother, smiling cheerfully as he looked upward. Oh, how beautiful was everything in the woods! All the trees were clothed in white; every little twig bearing shining points which glistened like gold.

"They are lighting up the Christmas trees for the children now," said Marietta, turning for a last look at the town; but in vain, for the windings of the road concealed it from her.

"Yes; but see here," said Anthony, pointing to the shining trees in the wood. And now suddenly they found themselves standing before a marvelous sight, that glittered with rainbow colors; it was the wood-brook, where it rolled from the mountain side, and stiffened under the icy breath of Winter.

There it remained hanging from twigs and stones in manifold beautiful forms; pearls, and points of hard crystal; each tiny drop reflecting the varied light of many stars. Never did Christmas table shine more beautifully. And above hung the silvered twigs of the fir tree, to which the heavens themselves had lent their light. It seemed as though the stars had come down to burn there as Christmas candles for the poor children. They stood, as if dazzled, before all this wondrous beauty.

"But, brother," Marietta exclaimed, "we have turned out of the road."

"Do you not see," he answered, still smiling as if with some deep, heartfelt joy, "that we are to keep Christmas too? I knew that the Christ-child would not forget to prepare it for us. It is for this we have come into the woods; in my heart I saw all this before."

And then he began to talk very earnestly to his little sister of all the glorious things he seemed to see in the mysterious brightness of the woods. Then the children were very, very happy. Marietta, too, saw with simple, childlike faith, all the lovely shapes and wonders her brother's words described, and their trusting young hearts celebrated Christmas Eve with more joy and blessedness than, perhaps, could be found elsewhere in the world.

Nor did they now forget that sweet Christmas carol which, last year, their mother had sung with them. They folded their hands, looked up to heaven through the parted branches above them, and sang with soft, happy voices, their hymn to the holy Saviour. The night seemed to grow brighter, and ever brighter, and the children fancied they heard a thousand silvery voices joining in their song, while the Star of Bethlehem shone above them. Then Marietta felt tired, and rested against her brother; who, with his still, cheerful face, was leaning against the trunk of a tree.

"I could sleep," said the little girl, "if I only had a bed."

"Come," said Anthony, throwing his arm around his little sister, "the infant Christ had no better one in the manger, and afterward, you know, He had not where to lay His head. Rest your little head on my bosom and sleep sweetly, for it is Christmas Eve." Then they both sat silent; once when Marietta moved, her brother asked:

"Do you feel cold?"

"No," she answered, "but the ground is hard."

"Think of the manger," said the boy.

And the children both went peacefully to sleep. But during the night, God's loving hand spread a pure, dazzling cover of snow over the earth, under which the Christmas lights and their young lives passed quietly away.

* * * * * *

Perhaps, dear children, you will not be willing to follow me again into the great town, which was such a solitary waste for the poor orphans, notwithstanding its many Christmas trees, its wealthy people, and its magnificent gifts. But I should like to tell you how the rich children, Leopold and Elmina, spent their Christmas, that you might pity them as I do.

On that Christmas Eve they received more presents than could be found in any other house in town, and their parlor was lighted by so many candles that one large fir tree could not hold them all.

But all this rich Christmas, could not make the children happy. They looked pale under the light of the Christmas candles, and turned wearily away from their surfeit of presents. They both sat, resting their heads upon their hands, chilled through, and complaining that the room was not light enough, and when they were found to be sick, and were put to bed, they talked in a strange, rambling manner. They imagined themselves wandering in a vast forest, where gigantic trees were stretching their long arms after them, and complained of lying in cold beds of ice and snow, for they were shaking with severe chills.

I cannot tell you much more about them. Once since that Christmas Eve, I have heard it remarked that there were but few happy days in the counsellor's house; at which I do not wonder very much.

But the children in the woods slumbered sweetly, until the Spring sun had kissed away the snow which lay upon them. Then very soon blossoms and leaves sprang up there, so tall and luxurious, that they rested well beneath them. Snow and flowers, alternately, made their grave, and never did mortal eye discover the place of their repose, by the wood-fountain.

But if you ask me who, then, beside them knew of the lovely Christmas Eve in the woods, I will tell you only—the angels.

Good-Friday.

THE LITTLE GARDEN OF THE CROSS.

IN the southern part of the German Fatherland, where steep rocks tower above delightful valleys, and rapid streams wind like silvery ribbons through the landscape, a little village lay concealed among the mountains.

Near this mountain-girt village was a small cottage, sheltered by an overhanging precipice, and shaded by the leafy roof of a large elm. It was probably the smallest and least pretentious dwelling in the place,—yet it is thither, my dear children, that I would lead you.

Father Holbert, the joiner, lived there with his five children, the dearest treasure he had on earth, since as he said, the Lord had called his faithful wife Martha home. It was these children who made their little home, scantily furnished as it was, and scarcely able to boast anything of value, so bright and gay,—they, with their five blooming faces, their rosy, laughing cheeks, and happy eyes.

My story, however, relates but little to the cottage itself; rather to the little garden which lay before it, which one would scarcely have regarded as belonging to a poor man, for there besides the joyful increase bestowed on all through His rain and His sunshine, God granted a special blessing on humble, pious diligence. In this garden might be seen the evidences of order, sobriety and faithful care; but

Story for Good Friday.

The symbol of His sufferings. p. 23.

THE LITTLE GARDEN OF THE CROSS. 25

why Father Holbert tended it with most particular love, I must tell you;—as well as the reason for its name:

"The little garden of the cross."

You well know, my dear children, what is our richest treasure. What we bear in our hearts through life, and what is our "comfort in life and in death." It is the CROSS,—the death of the cross which our Lord Jesus suffered for us. He has indeed gone back unto the glory of His Father. But His cross remains with us, the symbol of His suffering, by which He bore the penalty of our sins, and for the sake of which He is ever ready to remove our guilt, when we look up to the Crucified, and pray in His name, "Forgive us our debts!"

There is then in all the world no symbol higher, holier, or more beautiful than that of the love of God's only Son crucified; none before which we shed more heartfelt tears;—none before which we find self more abased; while yet there is none which symbolizes to the soul such blessed hope and confidence. For He who died on that cross for us, is ready to make us also the children of God.

This firm faith, this cherished hope, abode in Father Holbert's heart; and so it was, that of all his earthly possessions, he valued none so highly as a wooden symbol of the Crucified Saviour.

This had been left him by his father, who had also been a joiner. The father was acknowledged to have been a skillful workman; and this figure, which he had made, though to artistic eyes imperfect, was still sufficient to awaken the warm love and prayers of a faithful heart. So this wooden cross was ever regarded as the most sacred possession of the family, a remembrance of the love of God, in the grace of which they were born, and in the comfort of which they hoped to die.

But the cottage was too narrow and mean, too dark and poor, to receive this treasure; at least thus thought the pious man; so he gave it some finishing touches, chose a place for it in his garden, and built above it a little protecting roof.

There it stood, and for its sake, Father Holbert and the children tended the garden with constant and peculiar care. It was a thing well known, also, in the village, where Master Holbert, notwithstanding his poverty, was very highly esteemed; and the villagers often trod the narrow, rough, road that led to his dwelling, that they might glance at the blooming little garden, and the cross which stood there, before which, as is the custom in Roman Catholic countries, they would then make the Christian sign.

It was Good Friday, and all on earth was still. No fires burned on the hearths; no frolicsome children shouted before the doors; even in the churches, the sound of bells and of organ music was not heard. The very Spring winds, which usually came rushing and resounding over the earth, rejoicing in the new life which they bore upon their wings, seemed to-day more quiet. The mountain streams whispered softly down, and the wood-birds were hushed in their nests. The "Garden of the cross" stood arrayed in silent, solemn beauty. Primroses and imperial lilies displayed their glowing colors in the sunlight, and many of their lovely sisters were breaking from their swelling buds.

On this day, in token of their love for the dear Saviour, Father Holbert's children came to plant at the foot of the cross, the most choice and beautiful things they could find in their flower-beds, that there they might grow green and blossom, and bring their names in gracious remembrance before the Lord.

First came the dark-eyed, warm-hearted little Gertrude, bearing a rose-branch, whose large, rich flowers should look up to the cross like eyes full of the depth and ardor of love.

Elizabeth, her gentle and thoughtful sister, planted forget-me-not, that its blue, pleading eyes might express the prayer its name signifies.

The brothers Gottlieb and Treumund brought lilies and rosemary, emblems of the innocence of the Son of God, and the sufferings of His people. And all these were planted around the sacred shrine.

Only Rudhelm, the youngest, had nothing to bring from his little flower-bed, for it lay waste, and covered with weeds; he was a wild, rude boy, who had no love for the gentle care of flowers. So he planted a slip of ivy, which, with daring courage, he had brought down from a steep precipice among the mountains; but it seemed scarcely probable that this shoot, torn from the bare rock, would take root and thrive down here in the valley.

Father Holbert looked with thankfulness, and with a silent prayer, upon his children; from his heart, he exclaimed, "Lord, I bless thee!" but added, "For Thou wilt not that any of Thy creatures should be lost;"—while his gaze rested upon Rudhelm, whose stubborn disposition had already become a sore trouble to his father.

I can tell you but little of the years which, after this Good Friday, followed one another over the valley and little town,—over Father Holbert's family and the "Garden of the cross." Those years were all much alike. Spring came, clothing everything with verdure. Autumn winds swept by, and left all bare again. Winter strewed snow-flakes over the mountains.

All the children had grown up. Gertrude and Elizabeth were gentle, pleasant maidens, whose care made the little home comfortable, whose love brightened the fireside. Gottlieb and Treumund were apt, willing boys, their father's aids in his labors; and all were cheerful, loving children, the joy of his heart. And when each had done his part, then all looked devoutly to Heaven and prayed, "Forgive us our debts!" for their faith in the sin-atoning Love, was what made their daily work "holy and acceptable to the Lord."

Only still with Rudhelm, the wild Rudhelm, it was not thus; the more earnestly the entreaties of love were pressed upon him, the more resolutely his heart seemed closed against them; and when his father found it his duty to use severity towards him, the ungovernable boy would rush out among the turbulent children of the village, or away into the lonely mountain ravines, where nature was as rough and irregular as his untamed spirit. From these fool-hardy excursions he would often return with torn clothes and wounded limbs, but only to spurn the loving anxiety with which his father and sisters warned him against his evil course.

For a long time, the little village had seemed unnoticed by the world, and its peaceful inhabitants had not felt this to be a misfortune. They went to a neighboring town, from time to time, to purchase the necessaries of life, but ever brought back with them their wonted love for their own humble home. The valley was not always to continue in such quiet.

For some time, strangers had visited the place, whose savage countenances, heavy beards, and unusual language inspired the villagers with no small fear. There were, indeed, those who lent a willing ear to the conversation of these strange men, for they spoke of a golden future, when all should be fortunate, and wealth should abound. But there was so much of fire and bloodshed, so much hatred and blasphemy, mingled with their fine promises, that the better class of people turned from them, shaking their heads, unable to put the least faith in their golden prophecies.

Among those who soon became intimate with the strangers, was, alas! Rudhelm; and before very long, he could not be contented without their company. This made poor Father Holbert's hair turn gray with sorrow, for he well understood that these were godless men who despised the Commandments of the Lord, and whose actions were an abomination in His sight; and that their talk of freedom and brotherhood meant only robbery and murder. The father's house ceased to be

Rudhelm's home and shelter; he was seen only with these dangerous companions, and at last, he was gone, no one knew whither; and burning tears fell on Father Holbert's wasted cheeks, if any one chanced to inquire after his youngest son.

In the village, every thing was much changed. Here and there in the streets, one might always see little groups of people, telling each other of the fearful things they had heard were going on in the world: and before long, their hearts were filled with sorrow and mourning by a summons which called the young men to arms. Gottlieb and Treumund had to go as soldiers, and Elizabeth, who had for several years been the wife of a good young peasant, must also part with her husband. She went home with her two little children to Father Holbert and her sister Gertrude, in the little cottage under the old elm-tree, "close to the dear cross of Christ," she said, and wiped her gentle blue eyes.

Then came times of great distress to the humble village. The fearful reports that had reached the people, of wild hordes of men who were carrying fire, robbery, and bloodshed through the land, were only too true, and not even this secluded valley could escape its share of the tumult of war. Many cottages were burned down,—many grain-fields trampled by horses' hoofs: no such trouble had yet befallen Father Holbert, and the belief was current among the villagers, that God protected his home for the sake of his little "garden of the cross."

But far more bitter sorrow awaited him; sorrow that almost broke the poor father's heart. Only a few weeks after his sons had left him, a party of soldiers passed through the place, who brought to him the last greeting of his Gottlieb, who had fallen near Freiburg; and some time later, as some wagons were passing, laden with the severely wounded, a friendly neighbor who had been standing by the road, came to him and said, with sympathizing tears:

"Have courage, friend Holbert, it is the Lord who orders all for thee. I must tell thee that I saw thy Treumund on one of those wagons." Not a word did the old man speak; but that night, when the moon rose, he was not in the cottage; and his daughters knew that he passed the night in his little garden.

The evil and mischief in the world seemed without end or limit. It was as if hell had poured forth evil spirits, to lead men astray, and to make them waste and destroy one another in their wild fury. Not a few of the brave sons of the land, the valiant defenders of law and order in their country's service, fell, as had Gottlieb and Treumund, victims of this unhallowed civil war. At last, many who had been led astray by those evil, rebellious spirits, came to their senses, and perceived the wicked arts which had enticed them: and now their short-lived rage against law and authority, turned into bitter revenge against the men whose magnificent promises had betrayed them into wretchedness and misery. They were ready a thousand times to curse them; and in all the mountain country, there was scarcely a place where young and old did not take up arms against the rebels, who had called themselves the friends of the people. It was necessary, indeed, that they should defend their homes and property, for robbery and violence marked the freebooters' course, and not even the infant in its cradle was spared. No rumor was so fearful as that of their approach. All who were weak and defenceless fled before them, leaving the strong and able to take vengeance on the traitors.

Our little village, already so severely visited by the troubles of war, was several times thrown into confusion by reports of the advance of a band of outlaws; each time women and children fled and hid themselves in the mountains, until the alarm proved to be false. One day shots were heard among the mountains, and again resounded the terrible cry, "Freebooters! freebooters!" This time it was, indeed, true; far down in the valley waved the red flag, and whoever refused to follow it, they had heard, would be horribly butchered. Again women, children, and old men fled; among the rest went Gertrude and Elizabeth, with the little children.

Father Holbert had given them his blessing and bidden them go; but no entreaties could move him to flight; calm as ever, he gazed on the setting sun, whose rays gilded the little garden and the holy shrine. Then he closed the cottage door; and with the sound of gun-shots and of whistling bullets outside, he thought, amid his prayers, of his sons; not two left to him now—only one—the lost Rudhelm.

Meantime the peasants, well armed, had met the invaders, as they entered the village, and found themselves the superiors in numbers and strength. But the opposition of the savage band, so well practiced in desperate combat, was fierce and stubborn. By nightfall, however, the contest was decided, and the red flag was in the hands of the peasants who, their wrath still unappeased, hunted the scattered freebooters singly, like wild beasts, among the houses and hedge-rows of the village.

Amid this fearful confusion of flight and pursuit, of death and dying groans, still lay the little garden of the cross, a peaceful, quiet spot, while the silvery rays of the moon lighted up the cross of the Redeemer. But hark! a rustling in the bushes, and over the low wall springs a man in rapid flight; just behind him there is a flash, a report, and struck by the deadly ball, the outlaw sinks to the ground. No one followed him; perhaps respect for the little garden kept back the pursuer, or perhaps, indeed, it might have been a second shot, which fell by the garden wall; I cannot tell. I only know that the quiet, silvery moonbeams rested as before on the cross of the Crucified, and at the same time lighted a pallid brow, from which the blood was falling in heavy drops. The eyes were feeble and dim, but they wandered restlessly, as if seeking something; whatever the object was, that longing gaze found it, and there rested. What so attracted and held those dying eyes? It was the cross of our dear Saviour, lighted up by the moon. Before it stood roses, forget-me-nots, lilies, and rosemary; but close, close to the foot of the cross, and thence upward to the very head of the symbol, twined an ivy-vine, clinging firmly as it climbed. Thereon rested the eyes of the dying man. Deadly pallor spread over his features, and the feeble pulse seemed scarcely to throb, but hour after hour passed, and still death came not. God's all-pitying grace had a work yet to accomplish ere life should depart. He alone knoweth what passed in the soul of the dying man; the bright moon itself, which seemed peacefully watching him from above, could only have seen the wounded head bend to the earth, and the white lips move, till at last the weak arm clasped the foot of the cross. Yes, it was the same arm which had planted that ivy-twig, little then, and without a root, which no one thought would grow. Roses, and lilies, and the other flowers, had since bloomed, year after year; the ivy alone bloomed not, but it had clung closely to the cross, and climbed upward and hung thereon. Did the fervent prayers of Father Holbert bring from Heaven the dew of love which kept the little vine alive?

It was the hour of grace for Rudhelm; no more forsaken, he did not long pray alone; behind him the white-haired man stepped forth from the cottage, and raising his hands heavenward, said, as once on Good Friday long ago:

"I thank Thee, Lord, for Thou wilt not, that any of Thy creatures shall be lost."

So the father's loving arms once more received his son, and in his old home he tended him with watchful care, until it pleased the Lord of grace to give the penitent young man a blessed and peaceful departure, such as He ever grants to sinners who repent and turn unto Him. Even with grateful joy did Father Holbert stand by the death-bed of this, his last son, where also knelt the daughters, with Elizabeth's little sons, Gottlieb and Treumund. It seemed as though all his children were once more around him, for "according to his faith," had it been done unto him; and he now saw, what he had ever believed, that it was the Lord's will that none of his dear ones should be lost.

Not long did the old man's pious soul inhabit the frail and weary body; and before he closed his eyes in death, he expressed a wish to be buried in the little garden. There he now reposes, near the spot where his warmest love dwelt; the cross of the crucified Saviour. Roses, lilies, and the other flowers still bloom there in all their loveliness; but the ivy climbs ever higher and thicker, telling summer and winter, to all who will hear it, the precious story of the love of the Saviour, so rich in grace, who will not that the sinner shall be lost.

Good Friday and the cross with all its clustering memories ever point us to the saving grace of our Lord Jesus Christ, for all who cling by faith to Him!

Easter.

THE RESURRECTION MORNING.

IT was the Saturday between Good Friday and Easter Sunday; that twilight day upon which the shades of death would still rest unbroken, but for the first light of the Resurrection Morning, which we seem already to see in the East. A day, dear children, full of sorrow, yet full of hope, like the soul of man, when the light of grace is first dawning upon it, with the promise of deliverance from the darkness of sin.

The day itself, too, was like twilight. The gray light of early morning still lingered, although it was now mid-day, and the earth was gloomy and cheerless, for thick clouds hung their mourning drapery about the sun. The force of the March storm, under which the earth had trembled during Good Friday, had indeed abated at midnight, but it still swept in fitful gusts over the bare fields, and wailed in dirge-like tones between the high houses, and through the angular streets of the city which is the scene of our story. It was yet early in the year, and although Spring had already looked down with her bright eyes, and with friendly sunshine had called forth many gay blossoms, she seemed to-day to have taken flight; and the few who ventured abroad, hastened their steps to place the kindly shelter of the house-door between themselves and the cutting wind.

The city of which we speak was quite an old one, and had a grave and reverend appearance, like all that survives to tell us the story of past centuries. But there were streets in it through which it saddened one's heart to pass, they were so narrow and dark, and it was so easy to see that Misery and Poverty, rather than joyous Life, made their home there.

In one of those little streets stood a high, but half-ruined house, whose upper stories were so dilapidated that they could not be occupied. Indeed, one would have supposed that the house had no inmates at all, if the light of two dim candles in the room next to the entrance door, had not striven feebly with the gloomy daylight. But even here there was no sign of active life; ah, no! it was rather the chamber of death. In the middle of the floor, on wooden stools, stood a coffin, by which burned two candles; those still watchers of the dead, which by their gradually failing light, repeat to us that oft-learned lesson, that the earthly life of man is like a little flame, soon to be extinguished; coming with every passing moment nearer to its close.

Was there, then, no one to weep over this coffin, and to look with a survivor's agony for the moment when it should be borne away? Ah! yes, there was one in that room; a broken-hearted mourner indeed, though but a very little girl. It was little Magdalene, standing alone and silent by the coffin of her mother.

The poor child had shed so many tears that she could scarcely weep any more. Almost all her recollections of her mother, were of her sickness; by her bed of pain, Magdalene's childhood had passed without many joys; yet the little heart had been warmed and cheered every morning by the lovelight in her mother's eyes. But during this last winter the poor mother had suffered so much that the dim eyes and sorrowful features seemed no longer able to smile, though her heart still burned, as she lay there helpless, with anxious love for her child. Her grief was silent and wasting; and if any one chanced to visit the little chamber—physician, nurse, or a distant relative, who came, indeed, seldom, but still once in a while—little Magdalene ever heard it said that her mother would die. She prayed often and earnestly for her, but only that the good Lord would take away her terrible pain, for it was that which filled her little heart with such bitter sorrow; and now the Lord had granted her petition, and the sick woman slumbered peacefully, in eternal rest from suffering; but the child did not yet apprehend that; she only realized for the first time the presence of that death of which she had so often heard, and sank altogether under the fearful certainty. Motionless and silent, and at last even without tears, she had passed the days since that first terrible moment; she had looked on silently, when a black cover was laid over the beloved face; she had listened without emotion, when the relative, a severe woman, whom she could not love, told her that she would take her home with her. Only when the attempt to lead her away had really been made, she had opposed it so earnestly, and entreated so piteously, "Let me stay!" that at last the poor motherless child had been left alone.

And now came the dark-looking men, whose business it was to bear away the dead body to the church-yard. Few neighbors walked in the little procession; the poor woman had come to this strange street, a widow, and alone with her only child; soon she had lain down upon the sick bed, from which she never again rose. The friends of earlier and happier days were afar, or dead, or had forgotten her;

so that only the relative, who, without love, and with grudging hand, had dealt out the paltry support on which she and her little daughter had lived, appeared as a mourner. Yet one heart followed the coffin, which, young as it was, bore a world of sorrow for the dead. It was the little Magdalene, who would not be separated from her mother, and who stole quietly along after the men who were carrying her away, until they came to the church-yard, and had laid her in the grave.

It was with only a silent prayer,—for we will hope that those men, who stood with heads uncovered, beside the grave, were really praying,—that the poor woman was laid to rest. Magdalene closed her eyes; she could not look into the open grave; it seemed as though all hope, all happiness had forever vanished from her,—for those dull, hollow sounds that she heard, were of the earth that fell on her mother's coffin-lid. Unheeded by those who stood around, she sank unconscious behind a grave,—and when she awoke from that stupor of grief, all were gone, and the wind was sweeping dismally over the lonely grave-yard.

On the spot where they had buried her mother, rose a hillock of black earth, on which, black as the earth itself, stood a plain cross. Oh, what an unspeakably sad sight for Magdalene! She sat down on the grave, pressed her little face to the cold earth, and felt as if her heart must break, until at last God gave her tears again,—tears that could not be repressed. Then she observed, not far distant, another newly-made grave, but much smaller; and Magdalene understood that a child was buried there. Some one was kneeling by that grave, also: it was a man in black clothing, with pale, gentle features. He wiped his eyes as he arose, and went away without having noticed Magdalene.

"Oh," cried she, in her despairing grief, "Oh, darling mother, if I could lie down here too, beside thee! if that only were my grave!"

Then, in sudden terror, she imagined that Death was looking on her from all the graves that surrounded her, while he held her mother fast, fast in his cold arms, and with the mother, all that little Magdalene had ever known of joy or comfort in life,—never more to be restored to her. She sprang up, and fled affrighted from the silent, lonely church-yard, never slacking her pace until she found herself in the street, among the living. But all passed her by, for their thoughts and looks were engrossed by other objects than the little forsaken maiden, whom none knew. Little Magdalene's steps at last became more and more slow; she had recollected that she must think of a home and shelter for the future,—and as the house of her unkind relative rose before her thoughts, she felt an uneasy foreboding of trouble and pain awaiting her. From this feeling she could not free herself;—it pursued her until at last, her fear of entering that house became so great, that she stood still in the street, looking around, as if seeking shelter or deliverance.

"They will look for me!" she said to herself—"they will take me back to her! Oh, help me, good God! I am terribly afraid!"

Now she noticed that high dark walls were near her, which towered, with sky-pointing spires, far above all the surrounding buildings. It was the cathedral; it stood like a refuge and defence for all around it; and as the thought occurred to Magdalene, that they might be searching for her, she involuntarily drew back into the shadow of its walls. Then she perceived that the church door was standing open. Magdalene had never been in God's house, but at this first glance into the open door, such a strange feeling came over her, as if some one were waiting for her within, who could soothe and protect her, that the little maiden entered the great church without hesitation.

The light came softly into the vast building, through the many-colored panes of high Gothic windows. What a noble, what a glorious sight! As Magdalene looked around, she scarcely realized that she was quite alone, for all that surrounded her appeared like life, in many varied forms, yet all blended into one, rising heavenward, to the high vaulted ceiling, from which beautiful little angel faces looked forth among clouds. She was, however, really alone; the seats of the church, which were placed between curious ornaments of carved Gothic work, were all empty; the only breath that the child could hear, was the deep sigh which the sublime scene drew from her own little bosom. On she went, further and further, through the aisles of the church, stepping instinctively very lightly, not to disturb the solemn stillness of the place.

Suddenly she stopped before a large picture, which, although the evening was fast coming on, was still in a clear light, because it hung directly opposite one of the high windows. The picture represented a rocky cave, with several women standing before it, apparently in deep sorrow:—near them lay a stone with a broken seal, and on the stone sat the form of an angel, with a radiant countenance, and with snow-white garments flowing around him. Magdalene's eyes rested earnestly on this picture. The affliction of the weeping women recalled to her memory the bitter tears with which she herself had knelt at her mother's grave; yes, she was sure that this cave, also, must be a tomb! but it was open! it was empty!

"Can a grave, then, ever open?" she exclaimed, and thought of the cold, silent mound under which her mother lay. Oh, how gladly would she have questioned the angel, at whose heavenly appearance the women seemed terrified,—though he must have been telling them something very glorious and beautiful, for his hand was raised, and his eyes shone, as with some wonderful intelligence. Lost in contemplation, our little one remained before the mysterious picture; it seemed to her that she must abide here, if she would learn all that her whole soul was longing to know.

Now, already, the daylight looked in through the windows as if with half-closed eyes; the twilight shadows deepened, and lay mysteriously among the colonnades of the church. Slowly, darkness gathered over the picture, till only the bright form of the angel glimmered forth from the canvas. Still the child's questioning gaze was fixed upon it; still she could see the angel's snowy robe, but not yet could she understand his message. She had seated herself upon a little bench which stood in the shadow of a large column opposite the picture; it was in a small space enclosed by a lattice, which had formerly been a pew; and while she still watched the glimmer of the white robe, she fell asleep; yes, sweetly asleep, though she was alone in the broad, high church. Yet *not* alone, for in a lovely dream the Lord sent His angel to her.

It seemed to Magdalene that she sat again by the side of her sick mother, the eyes of the sufferer resting as ever, with earnest love, upon her child. It must have been a sweet memory that visited her on the wings of her dream; for now she heard from those loved lips the wondrously beautiful story of the Resurrection of Christ; even as her mother had once related it to her. "I live, and ye shall live also," Jesus had said. Those words her mother seemed to repeat, and smiled sweetly, as though she would have added, "So also *I* live, and we shall meet again." Then she would have embraced her mother, but as she stretched her arms toward her, she receded farther and farther, yet still looking on the child with the same loving smile. But when little Magdalene would have risen and followed her, she suddenly seemed to be standing, as she had on the day before, weeping bitterly by a silent grave; then the angelic figure, which had sat by the tomb of the Lord, approached her—the being whom her suffering heart had questioned, without understanding his message—and now, now she comprehended all; so far her dream.

The light finger-tips of slumber rested now only upon her eyelashes; her eyes, already but half closed, opened quickly at that moment; Magdalene was awake. Sunshine, golden Easter sunshine, flowed through the church, filling it with radiance; rich waves of organ music, glorious as the roar of the sea, poured forth in a grand song of victory; "Christ is risen," sounded from a thousand voices. The little maiden sank on her knees, and as the picture of the Resurrection shone in the glowing rays of the Easter morning sun, so also was her young soul filled with light and glory by the faith of the Resurrection. "Christ is risen," she also sang, recalling, by a marvel of memory, the words of the beautiful song, which she had once heard her mother read aloud. And

Story for Easter Morning.

"*Christ is Risen*" sounded from a thousand voices. p. 60.

her voice was borne upward with those of the thousands who were singing with her; for a multitude of worshipers filled the church, as far as Magdalene, from her hiding place, could see.

But now the song was hushed, and the attention of the devout hung breathlessly upon the words of the preacher, who entered the pulpit, and in language of inspiring eloquence, proclaimed the Resurrection of our Saviour. He spoke of the victory, the peace, the hope of Easter morning.

"Christ, arisen from the dead, hath vanquished death; and we conquer with Him. Christ, arisen from the dead, said to His disciples—'Peace be with you,' and upon us also He sheds His peace. Christ, arisen from the dead, gives us the hope of eternal life; and with it the hope of reunion with those we have loved and lost."

And now the voice of the speaker became tender and full of emotion; and when he recounted the loved ones whom God calls home to Himself, it trembled as with irrepressible tears. But he had spoken words full of power to comfort the heart of Magdalene, the poor little orphan, and she looked up with real heartfelt trust to the man who seemed as confident of the joys of Heaven, as if he had been there. She thought sometimes that she had seen that pale, gentle face before, whose very expression was so soothing to her that with regret she saw him at last descend from the pulpit, and disappear from her gaze among the crowd of worshipers. Now again the organ poured forth its flood of harmony, and the congregation sang "Praise to Him, Death's mighty Conq'ror." Then from the altar the preacher spoke the benediction; the joyful, solemn Easter blessing, elevated and sustained by which, the crowd left the house of God.

Magdalene had not yet returned to the consciousness of her lonely condition; she had seemed raised above hunger and weakness, until now, as she was about to be left alone again in the mighty church, which the crowd of worshipers had already quitted. She heard the sound of a single step, coming along the pillared aisle; and, as she came out from her little hiding-place, she saw that it was the preacher; yes, she beheld again those kindly features on which she had looked with so much pleasure during the sermon. When the clergyman saw the little girl standing by the column, he stopped and looked lovingly at her, though his lips quivered sorrowfully, as he said:

"Did you come alone to church, dear child?"

Then little Magdalene took courage,

and told him all her sad story, as she could have related it to none other in the wide world; and while she spoke, tears stood in the minister's eyes.

"I also had a child," he said; "a little daughter, lovely as you are, and looking like you; the Lord, who gave her to me, hath soon taken her away; only yesterday I laid her in the grave. Little Magdalene, in you God hath given me another child; will you be my daughter?"

The child clung to him, feeling that she could love him, as she never had loved any but her mother; even as she might have clung to her father, had she ever known him. And now, too, she was certain that this was not the first time she had met him; but that he was the same whom she had seen bending over the child's grave.

Although still young in years, the clergyman, who was a man of faith and love, a true disciple of Jesus, had drained many a cup of sorrow; had borne, in the strength of the Lord, much grief and pain, for he also was alone on earth, having early followed all his dear ones to the grave. He took Magdalene to his own home, and from the day when God's hand thus led them together, these two never again separated.

And whenever the beloved Easter Festival returned, they went together at the earliest dawn to the church-yard, and there at the graves of their loved ones, by the rising Easter sun, celebrated the Resurrection morning.

Heaven-Keys.

A STORY FOR ASCENSION DAY.

THE sun of Ascension Day was already giving his farewell greeting to the pleasant valley, so protectingly surrounded by green hills, and the warm May day had yielded to the cold freshness of evening, when, on the top of a steep height, from which a slender cross looked seriously down into the green depth below, a cheerful little group sat engaged in familiar conversation. It was a mother with her two children, as one might be assured by a glance at the middle-aged woman and at the blue-eyed, fair-haired young creatures at her feet, upon whom she looked as only a mother can look at her darlings. And he who sat at her side, the tall man in black clothing, with the sonorous voice and the ardent heart, to which his words bore witness, as did the glistening sparks that flashed so beautifully among the fresh verdure of the spring foliage to the work carried on in the valley below; that man was the shepherd of the little flock in the valley, who led them in green pastures and by quiet waters, for—

"There is our pastor, who is so very good to us," was the remark of a peasant in a blue blouse, who was at that moment leading a party of strange ladies and gentlemen up the dizzy height, near our little group.

The pastor was the friend of the mother and her children, and had invited them on that pleasant festival evening, to go out with him into the great, wide, verdant, and blooming temple of the Lord, after having twice borne witness to the Heaven-ascended Redeemer in his stone church in the valley.

Erna, the little girl, had long waited impatiently for a pause in the conversation of her mother and their friend, and at last holding up a bunch of golden-yellow cowslips, (called in that region *Himmel-schluessel* or Heaven-keys), she asked:

"Dear pastor, what is the reason for this name of 'Heaven-keys?'"

First casting his eyes downward for a moment in quiet thought, the pastor looked quietly at Erna, and her brother Walter, in whose earnest eyes he read the same question the sister had spoken, and said:

"The answer to your inquiry might furnish material for a story on our way homeward. Shall I?" he added, addressing the mother as she rose from her mossy seat.

"I beg for the story for myself and my children," she replied. So their friend presently began thus:

"It is a legend handed down to us from the past, and which leads us so far back that it is difficult to determine whether it springs from the soil of truth or of fable; in any case it is so beautiful that one is not unwilling to believe it, and so touching that it cannot but affect our hearts.

"We all know the pleasant meadowland, surrounded by thick trees, which lies a league from here, and is called Heaven's Gate. There, long before those trees were yet young saplings, a century before our grandparents had seen the light of life, a merry group of children played, and looked into the windows of the ancestral castle, gilded by the sunlight; but the castle was then no ruin. The thoughtful Alma, the pastor's gentle, blue-eyed little daughter, was, though unconsciously, the life of this little party of children. Her bright, soulful eyes discovered the most beautiful flowers for their fragrant garlands; her clear voice led the rest in the sweetest melodies; from her glowing fancy sprang the most charming stories; and withal, all that she did was most gentle and childlike. At times she stole away swiftly from the lively players, and, it would seem, went to some secluded place to catch fresh sunlight for her golden hair and blue eyes, for ever more lovely she came back from her retirement to the living garland of children around her. They could not long do without her, their white rose; so with quick eyes her playful companions watched for her, and gaily welcomed her back, as at last she returned to them with a cluster of these golden stars glittering on their green stems.

"Alma! come, let us play," they all shouted, as with one voice; but Alma shook her sunny head and sat down in the springing grass, looking fixedly into the golden chalices of the starry flowers. Directly, as though they had silently answered some question for her, or conveyed some new idea to her perception, she sprang lightly up again, beckoned to the children to follow her, and, accompanied by the willing crowd, she hastened from the green meadow to an oak; which spread its knotty branches abroad at no great distance from them. Arrived under it, the children stopped, and Alma, standing in the midst of them, said with crimsoned cheek and fluttering breath:

"'Listen! I have had a dream. I was standing in a beautiful garden; there were no roses nor lilies in it, no wall-flowers nor lark-spur; but from all the beds these golden flowers were nodding to me, and the paths were strewn with them, and a delicate figure in a white mantle was crowned with them; and she came to me and placed a wreath on my head too, and said, 'Alma, this is a heavenly garden, and these flowers are called Heaven-keys.' Just as she said this she disappeared, and the garden too, and the whole dream; but I cannot forget it; and a little while ago, when I was gathering these flowers, it seemed to me all the while as though they must be telling me some secret, and so I listened; but they were silent, until I came back to you, and sat down in the grass with my flowers; then it seemed as if something began to sound in the depth of their yellow cups, and told me what I should do. That is the reason why I came here, and called you to come with me, for now I am going to climb this oak, higher and higher, from one branch to another, until I reach the top where that green spray touches the soft, white cloud; and I will take the prettiest of the flowers

Story for Ascension Day.
"These flowers are called Heaven-Keys." p. 72.

with me, and open Heaven with it for you and me, for they are Heaven-keys, you know; so, then, we can all go to the lovely, sweet Heaven, where our dear Lord Jesus will watch over us, and the angels will play with us. I pray every evening, "Dear Lord make me holy, that I may come to Thee in Heaven." And now I know how I can go there, and become true and holy. When I have opened the gate, I will go right in; if you will only stay here I will call and tell you how pleasant it is, and I will say to one of the angels:

"I pray thee, dear angel, go down and bring up the other children, for the oak is such a steep ladder." And then we will play together in Heaven, and listen to the kind Saviour, while He tells us how we may become holy; and then we will all give Him our hands, and say:

"Farewell, dear Lord Jesus, we will soon come back." Then we will all come down again, and this evening when mother puts me to bed, and says, 'God bless thee, dear child,' I will put my arms round her neck and say, "Dear mother, now I shall be very holy, for I have been with the dear Jesus."'

"Silent and astonished, the children listened to Alma's words. Elsie, her dearest companion, then fastened the prettiest blossom from her bouquet in her fair hair, that she might not lose it in her steep upward journey; and with her aid the dear child sprang to the lowest limb, then, wearied already, but with great agility, she climbed further, now and then casting loving, happy looks on those below. But—oh sorrow! she made one false step; her little, delicate hands were not able to grasp a strong bough that offered its help just above her; one instant more, and the white rose lay pale and broken on the ground, by the trunk of the oak, the golden star still in her streaming hair. The young playfellows stood weeping around the little child of Heaven; but the mother, who had been called, knelt silently at her side. Once more the little creature feebly opened her eyes, sought with her hand for the blossom in her hair, folded it in her hands over her heart, gently moved her lips, and only the mother's listening ear caught the words, 'That I may come to Thee in Heaven.' One more breath, and all was still; Alma's soul was with her Saviour; her dear little form lay dead. Amid prayers and tears she was laid in the still, cool grave; her father chose as his funeral text, 'Suffer little children to come unto me, for of such is the kingdom of Heaven.' Her mother planted the golden flowers on the little grave; and since that time every one here has called them Heaven-keys."

Here the pastor ended his story, and

the mother's eyes were moist and shining, as she drew her two children nearer to her, while they pressed tenderly to their mother's side. They were passing before the village graveyard, just as the story of Alma was finished, and on nearly all the graves, cowslips were blooming; here under a white cross, there on a fresh mound; in the sleeping bed of the infant child, as on the resting-place of the world-weary old man. They lingered a moment before the iron gate. The pastor clasped his hands, glanced upward, and said:

"Lord, grant to all of us the true key of Heaven. Amen."

Silently they went on, and separated with an affectionate pressure of the hand, under the shade of the lindens before the parsonage. But the mother and her children were quiet and serious all that evening. The merry Erna cared not for jest or sport; and little Walter looked as he

A STORY FOR ASCENSION DAY. 77

always did at church. They both sat down with their mother at the house-door, and talked of Benno, their happy brother, to whom, only one year before, the Saviour had opened the door of Heaven.

Whitsunday.

THE LITTLE APOSTLE.

THE lovely days of May had clothed the earth in its sun-bright, flower-embroidered garments, and poured out all the wealth of Spring beauty over mountain and valley, field and plain. The young foliage still wore its tenderest, brightest green, unsullied and fresh as when the first sunbeam glanced upon it, struggling forth from its enveloping buds; and the grain-fields were spread like a soft, green carpet over the hills which stretched along the margin of the river.

Who can name all the living creatures which breathe the delicious vernal air, and bear, each in its own way, their parts in the vast anthem of praise, earth's Hallelujah Chorus to the Lord? Who can count the flowers, which, silently called forth, spring up in their loveliness to solemnize the new creation of Nature? Ah, my children, Earth has room for endless beauty and joy,—but the heart of man is too weak to comprehend it all, and seems as though it must burst with the pressure of newly awakened life and joy.

The beautiful picture of Spring, which we have here tried to describe, was mirrored in the eyes of a boy, who sat on the ridge of a hill, looking thoughtfully into the far distance. It was little John, an orphan boy. The brother of his early-departed mother had taken him to his own home, to bring him up with his two sons. Mr. Siegmund, that was his uncle's name, loved him fondly, for he traced in the boy the gentle spirit of his mother, whose memory was dear to his heart: indeed, his heart turned almost unconsciously, with more tenderness to this child of his sister, than to his own sons, by whom he had ever been less appreciated, less beloved and respected than by the tender, loving little John.

More than once, indeed, had quite dark clouds gathered in the sky of their household peace, because Francis and Ferdinand looked with jealous eyes upon the adopted boy, who stood nearer than they to their father's heart.

So far from acknowledging their little cousin's superiority to be the cause of this, they suspiciously fancied that he designed, by winning their father's affection, not only to lessen their paternal inheritance by division with him, but even to supplant them entirely, and so gain all for himself.

Oh, what base, perverted thoughts does envy implant in the heart of man! How little did they understand the pure and innocent mind of the orphan boy, who had never thought of any possession on earth so desirable as a loving heart! He could not but see that his uncle's sons morosely avoided him, and sometimes even mocked him, and sought to distress him: this only made him turn the more lovingly to his kind uncle, leaving the two boys, who were much older than himself, to go their own ways, without cherishing any resentful thoughts of the insults he had endured from them.

Mr. Siegmund always had some comforting words for him, if only Francis and Ferdinand were not present,—for even he feared the unkind treatment of his sons, though he had always been an affectionate father,—only too weak and indulgent.

Mr. Siegmund was full of kindness and benevolence towards all; if those around him were happy, his own cheerful spirit rejoiced with them; and it was ever his pleasure to wipe away the tears of sorrow. Never a day passed on which the needy did not seek his door; and when they did not come to ask aid, his beneficence found out their needs, and many a warm pot of soup, and much relief, in money and in clothing, were carried from his house into the dwellings of the sick and the poor. In these merciful works John was like another pair of hands to him. He had a peculiar aptness for finding those who were in want, and was never more happy than when his father, as he called Mr. Siegmund, entrusted any such commission to him. So he was frequently seen leaving the house with the rapid step of one bent on a pleasant errand of love, his hands never empty; and so well did the neighbors know him as the help-bearing messenger of Mr. Siegmund, that they took pleasure in calling him "the Little Apostle." His cousins also, Francis and Ferdinand, gave him that name, but only in scornful mockery, for they thought his interest in the poor to be artfully assumed, in order to gain their father's partiality, and besides they were so stingy that they could not bear to see so much given away.

On the day when we first met little John, he was returning from a visit to a sick person, who lived half a league from the town, and to whom he had carried some strengthening food. It was a walk in which he always took particular pleasure, not only because the road wound along so pleasantly over hills and through meadows, but because the old man to whom he had carried the food, was so dear to him. It was Father Everard, who had always delightful conversation, or beautiful stories for his young visitor, although he had long been confined to his bed.

To-day it was Ascension-Day. John had lingered for more than an hour, and while the old man was eating his soup, had taken up the large illustrated Bible that lay on the table by his bed. It was not the first time the boy had held the sacred Book, while the old man related its histories to him: on this day he sought out the picture of Christ's Ascension, and gazed, as if he could not bear to lose sight of it, at the beloved figure of the Saviour, borne away upon light clouds, vanishing upward from the longing eyes of His disciples.

All the events in our Lord's earthly history passed through the boy's mind; His sufferings, death and resurrection, as the pious Everard had related them; and lastly the forty days during which the risen Master walked with His disciples, those forty days which Nature still yearly celebrates, adorning them with all her earliest loveliness. Indeed, the picture was one, which might well call up solemn and beautiful thoughts; it showed the Lord carried on the cloud, up toward a glorious ray of everlasting light, which broke forth from the gates of Heaven, opened to receive their King, now returning unto the glory of His Father, as the Conqueror and Ruler of the world. It seemed consoling to little John, when he thought of the bitter sufferings and death to which Christ's boundless love had brought Him down, to remember that the Redeemer had returned to His Father, and His own glorious Home, never again to taste the cup of sorrow, nor to suffer death by murderous hands. But when he looked again at the disciples, and saw how sorrowfully they gazed after their Lord, it appeared to him that the pain of their loneliness must have been something like that of a weak child, when its mother's tender supporting arm is withdrawn. He said so, in simple, childish language, to his old friend, who replied:

"Once, when the Lord had foretold His departure to His disciples, and their hearts were full of sorrow at His words, He said, 'If I go away, I will send the Comforter to you; the Spirit of Truth, who will guide you into all truth.' Then He added, 'I have yet many things to say unto you, but ye cannot bear them now.' How is it, my little John," continued Everard; "can *you* bear them yet? But the day will come for you as for the disciples; ah, my son, I should love dearly to keep Whitsunday with you," and the old man's eyes grew bright and earnest.

"Good Everard, tell me these things, for I do not know them," answered the boy; "yes, I will come again on Whitsunday, and then you will explain this to me."

"Knowledge, interpretation," said the old man, half to himself, shaking his head thoughtfully; "yes, come again, but soon; for my days are almost numbered."

Little John's thoughts were still dwelling on this conversation, when he looked from the hill where we first saw him at the sunset. The horizon was like a sea of fire, in which the sun's last rays were already disappearing. Clouds had rolled together to veil his departure, and surrounded him as with a gold-bordered diadem. John thought of the Ascension of the Lord, but as yet he saw only the clouds in which He had disappeared, and not the bright crown which He reaches forth from above to His own.

Scarcely two days had passed, when John again visited Father Everard's cottage. The old man's strength was fast failing, but he still smiled pleasantly when he saw the boy, and said, pointing to the Bible, which lay open before him:

"You see I was expecting you."

Then he asked John to read the second chapter of Acts, in which St. Luke describes the pouring out of the Holy Spirit; and himself added the history of the ministry and miracles of the Apostles. The boy was deeply moved by the recital.

"Oh," cried he, "if I could but follow the good Apostles, that by me too the Lord would add to the Church such as should be saved."

"It is the gift of God," returned the old man; "but he who receives does so that he may give it again. Be still before the Lord, John, your hour will come."

But John was absorbed in his own thoughts. A wish for the future had been formed in his heart; a purpose which, from that time, he never gave up. As soon as he reached home, his thoughts arose to his lips, and his good uncle learned his ardent desire to devote himself to sacred studies, so that he might become a servant of the Word, to proclaim the precious gospel.

But where the Lord is pleased to bestow the might of His Spirit, there He first breaks the reigning power of self; and so little John must first pass through bitter trials before he could be comforted with that joy of the Holy Ghost, which should abide with him thenceforward forever. Several days after, as he was returning from another visit to Father Everard, he met Mr. Siegmund, who appeared much agitated.

When John anxiously inquired the cause, his uncle answered him in a rough tone, quite unusual with him, but only assumed to conceal his deep emotion:

"John, the peace of my house is gone; we must part."

A sad scene had taken place during John's absence. Francis and Ferdinand had heard of his desire to devote himself to the holy ministry, and at once imagined this to be an artful design of his to raise himself above them; besides, the idea of the great expense his education would require, filled them with spite and ill-will. They urged their weak father with reproaches and threats, until he yielded and promised that John should be bound as apprentice in another town, to learn a trade as his own father had done.

The poor boy stood as if struck dumb, when he heard all this from his kind benefactor, and found that in a few days he must leave his home to learn his father's trade.

Poor John; all his bright hopes were gone. But now he had imagined himself a servant of the Church; a preacher of the Word; and this must be given up, and he must leave his kind, fatherly protector, for the dark workshop of a shoemaker. His heart seemed almost broken; he sought in vain for comfort. But while he wept silently, alone by the window of his own little room, he thought of the words of his gray-haired friend:

"Be still before the Lord, John."

Whitsunday came, and joy seemed spread over all the earth. The butterfly flitted from flower to flower, and, with still richer delight, the lark soared toward heaven. But one came forth from the dark prison of city-life, by whom all Nature's loveliness seemed unperceived, for his downcast eyes were often filled with blinding tears. It was John; and he was going to take leave of Father Everard, for on the next day he was to leave Mr. Siegmund's house. As he entered the house a kind woman, who was nursing the old man, met him with a sad look, and said:

"Go in, my good boy, and take my place for the next hour; his end cannot be far distant."

John went to the bedside; the old man could not move; but his eyes beamed with pleasure, and with a sweet, peaceful smile, he said:

"See, my son, we shall still keep Whitsunday together."

Silently, but full of sympathy, he listened to the orphan boy's story of his disappointment and trouble; then he said to him:

"John, those whom the Holy Spirit leadeth, are the children of God; can you desire more? Pray for His Spirit, so shalt thou receive from His fulness, grace for grace. Do not wish to anticipate God's time; for the fruit of the Spirit is not only love, joy, and peace, but also patience. Pray with me for the Pentecostal blessing, my son; pray in humility and faith; the Lord will not refuse your petition."

The window of the little room was open, and the blossom-laden branches of the apple tree that overshadowed the cottage, waved into the chamber of death. The gentle fragrance of Spring pervaded its atmosphere, while, hidden in the topmost boughs of the tree, a nightingale sang in soft, mellow notes. During the quiet hour of prayer, her song was hushed, and not until the stars appeared in the twilight did it commence again, soft and clear as ever, before the window of the dying old man.

Not much earlier than this had John left his friend's side; and what gift those last hours had brought for him; how the

Spirit of the Lord had been poured out upon him; ah! my children, what words can express this holy mystery? But clothed with power from on high, the boy left the cottage, and when he reached his home, all wondered to see his countenance shine with such quiet inward joy.

Two or three days had passed, and John was now no more in his uncle's house, his childhood's home. He had left without bidding farewell to Mr. Siegmund, for when he went to take leave of him, he found his door locked. But when he unpacked the few things he had brought with him to his master's house, he found among them a Bible and hymn-book, and recognized his uncle's hand in the trembling lines in which his name was written in them.

Mr. Siegmund's neighbors looked in vain for the "Little Apostle;" the poor waited longer than ever before at his door; and he himself, who had ever been so cheerful, was now often gloomy and sad. His sons both became merchants, and lived near their father; but since they had driven away his little John, their mutual confidence was almost destroyed. After some time, the boy was removed to a town still more distant, to the care of another master. It was said that this also was through his cousins' interference; worse still, the letters that he wrote to his fatherly benefactor, seldom reached him. So passed a number of years, during which he never returned to his old home, and at last, but few remembered "the Little Apostle," whom they had formerly taken such pleasure in seeing.

* * * * * *

In the year 1832, the Asiatic Cholera first visited the northern part of Germany. Its appearance was the herald of Death, and all horrors were in its train, but most terrible of all was the shuddering fear which made the earth seem a vast charnel house, and the living like walking corpses. We follow the disease into the town which has been the scene of our story. Over it also had spread those horrors which, like an inexorable judgment, had travelled from East to West. After the people had long watched its gradual approach with constantly increasing anxiety, one morning the fearful words were suddenly heard:

"The Cholera is here!" and like a band of iron, under which ruddy Life whitens, stiffens, and at last grows cold in Death, the news fell upon the whole town.

An awful stillness reigned. Scarcely dared any one leave his house; each dreaded to greet his neighbor, lest in so doing, he should receive the gift of Death;

only here and there one might see solitary figures, hurrying along, with all the fearfully suggestive signs of precaution against infection.

In one street, particularly, no one had been seen since morning; the house-doors were fast locked, and none looked from the windows: it was here the cholera had first appeared. All had been thus deserted from morning until noon, when suddenly the sepulchral stillness was broken by the rapid steps of a youth, hastening alone in this street of death.

Without pause or hesitation, he approached a house at the corner of the street. Now he has reached the door, will he not shrink back? Above it, on a black tablet, are the words: "The cholera is here!" But he does not shrink; indeed, he seems to have been fully prepared for this, for he rings impatiently, and when admitted, hurries past the few lonely watchers, to a well-known chamber. Through the darkness of the room, dim with the smoke of fumigation, he recognizes the sick man's features; he opens his arms, and the dying Siegmund lay on the bosom of his John.

The disease of which he was the first victim, had already almost finished its rapid course; the signs of death were upon his features, but their stiff rigidity relaxed into a sweet, peaceful smile, as he looked once more upon the beloved son of his sister. So at last they met, these two who so dearly loved each other, but whom the restless spirit of Envy had so long separated.

But God's Spirit is the Conqueror of all others, and Mr. Siegmund's last, imploring words were:

"John, forsake not my poor sons!"

When the young man had closed the eyes of his fatherly friend, and was leaving the house where he lay in the calm repose of peace, he observed two persons who drew back in affright as he opened the door. It was Francis and Ferdinand, who, in cowardly fear, hovered around the house where their father lay, without daring to enter. When they recognized "the Little Apostle," ill-will and avarice again arose in their hearts, struggling with the fear of death, and they cast upon him a look of the bitterest hatred.

"He has come at the last hour," they said, "to steal away our inheritance." Ah, they little suspected that their dying father had entreated John for their sake, that he, truly rich in the Spirit of the Lord, would have pity on their poverty.

* * * * * *

It was on Ascension-Day 18—, that a crowd of people thronged the streets near the river, in the city of Bremen. An emigrant ship was to sail at noon, and no observing eye could watch without interest, the various groups gathered there. It seems to me that the lot of the emigrant is one of perpetual sorrow; it is as though one should tear a tree by its roots from the ground, to plant it, all uncertain of its thriving in a strange region. But the many different countenances gathered around this ship, did not, generally, wear an expression of sadness; one might see rather indifference, expectation, or restlessness, painted there; but then, the sorrowful moment when the home shore disappears from the gaze, had not yet come.

Some powerful, mysterious, though far distant, attraction must have beckoned onward this crowd of people. There were grey-haired men, whose years must have been almost numbered, who yet turned westward with looks of anticipation; there were young mothers, who fearlessly confided themselves and their tender, delicate infants to the rough elements, willingly exchanging their native hearth, for uncertain happiness in a foreign country.

Among these varied groups was one countenance, which attracted frequent attention. It was that of a young man, in plain black dress, with fair hair, parted above his forehead, and delicate features, wearing an expression of peace and joy. He was the centre of a little group, who were listening with earnest attention to his words. They were those in whose eyes tears of regret stood, and whose hearts beat ever more painfully, as the hour of departure drew near.

"Who is the young man, that is talking with those emigrants?" asked one bystander of another.

"He is a missionary," was the reply. "I heard him relate his story a little while ago. It is not long since he was a simple shoemaker's apprentice. He won the affection of a clergyman in the town where he lived, who instructed him, and assisted him in carrying out his design of devoting himself to the ministry. By this clergyman's aid, he went to Basle, to prosecute his studies, and now he is going out in the emigrant ship to North America, in order to be sent thence as a missionary to China."

The embarkation had now begun. The given signal, the roar of a cannon, burst forth from the ship, and the first boat pushed off from the land, followed by many parting salutations. It was long before the gangway was clear of the ascending passengers. Just as the last seemed to have entered, a boat, which had been detained, was hastily moved up alongside of the ship.

Two men stepped from it, followed by a young woman, with a child in her arms. The young man, pointed out as a missionary, had been standing by the head of the gangway, watching those entering the vessel, with great attention.

But as this last boat lay by the ship, and its passengers came from it, a sudden paleness overspread his face, and, as if he would conceal it, he bowed over the side of the deck, toward the swelling waves. But tears arose to his eyes, and a slight motion of his lips permitted one to suspect whither his spirit had directed itself.

Favoring winds carried the vessel in the shortest possible time, across the channel, past the English coast, and out into the wide open sea. Then a calm ensued. A sky in which, as far as the eye could reach, no cloud could be perceived, spread out above the ocean; and the sails hung loosely from the mast.

This, however, did not continue long. By morning, the air seemed filled with a strange, confused sound, while the plain of the sea still lay motionless: the crew were stirring restlessly to and fro, while the captain's glass was steadily directed towards a place in the horizon from which a high cloud was rising. The cloud formed itself into a dark column, which spread out broader and broader, above the waters, and scarcely had the words: "We shall have a storm!" been pronounced, when the vessel was flying along, more and more rapidly as the wild tossing of the billows increased. At this intelligence, a cry of terror sounded through the hold, where the emigrants had crowded closely together for shelter.

But the howling of the storm, and the raging of the deep, soon drowned every complaint. One moment they were borne high on the foaming crest of a wave, with a deep, black abyss yawning before them, into which the roaring hurricane seemed to plunge itself, as though it must reach the very bottom of the sea; and in the next instant, the unfortunate vessel swung down after it into the fearful gulf. But quickly the storm seized it as with a mighty hand, and set it on high, when the dashing wave seemed to flutter and foam in the very face of the heavens.

The poor ship seemed only the forlorn prey, over which the monsters of the deep roared and fought. Then through the black night of clouds, quivered a flash of lightning, and a second followed it, the cleft mainmast fell upon the deck, and flames burst forth in the stern of the vessel.

Oh, how frightful was this tumult of elements, warring among themselves, but all united against those miserable beings, who climbing from plank to plank, contended for life until the last moment! Who can paint their misery, what words can express their desperation?

Amid all these deathly horrors, the figure of the missionary was seen clinging closely to the forward mast. The young man's eyes glowed with spiritual light; his words, the words of prayer, died away unheard, but he spoke to the little party who crowded closely around awaiting death with him, in looks that told the victory of faith. Then came a mighty wave, that seemed about to take the very heavens by storm; it cast the ship on a sand-bank, and itself falling on the blazing part, extinguished the flame. But at the same instant, a sound, like a far-off, wailing cry, rolled through the storm; it was the death-shriek of more than a hundred unfortunates, who swept from the deck, found their grave in the flood.

Then the youth, forgetting his own peril, raised both hands toward Heaven, as though he must bring thence, pity for

Story for Whitsuntide.

"Were floating over the wide, lonely ocean." p. 107.

the souls struggling in death, and from his lips resounded the cry, "Come, Holy Spirit!" And the storm bore the words upon its wings, and high in the air, and low in the deep, amid the dying, re-echoed the prayer, "Come, Holy Spirit!"

On the following day, the emigrant ship was a forsaken wreck, washed by the waves; but the little company who were saved from death, had entrusted themselves to a small boat, and were floating over the wide, lonely ocean. They were about twenty in number, and among them was the youthful missionary.

I need scarcely say, that in him we have found John once more, "the Little Apostle," to whom Father Everard had once said, "Be still before the Lord, John, thine hour will come!"

Francis and Ferdinand, who, discontented with themselves and with all that surrounded them, had left their home as emigrants, and by God's providence had been led to the same vessel with John, had not recognized him. They knew nothing of the change in his circumstances, and, therefore, were far from expecting to find him in the missionary, whom during their journey they had studiously avoided, because his countenance, by some strange, but to them unaccountable resemblance, seemed to convey to their consciences a continual reproach.

But the hour of recognition had come. The young wife of Ferdinand had perished in the storm, and Death had stretched forth his hand to seize the brothers also, but at the last moment, they had been drawn almost senseless, into the boat. When the younger brother again opened his eyes, the missionary, with a look of unspeakable love, laid the child whom he himself had saved into his arms.

The burning tears which Francis and Ferdinand shed before him whom they had once so bitterly hated, he pleaded as offerings of penitence, in silent intercession before God. "John, forsake not my unhappy sons!" had been the dying father's entreaty, and the Lord had enabled the young man to fulfill the promise he had made.

Three days passed, and the boat still floated lonely upon the sea; the little crew had no food to sustain life; but John ever soothed them with the precious words of the Gospel, and the Spirit of God was with him.

At last a white sail glimmered in the horizon. An hour of fearful suspense followed. The ship of which they had just caught a glimpse seemed to direct her course from them, and they were still desolate and forsaken. But the watchful eye of God was upon them, and the moment of deliverance was not far distant.

The wind now suddenly changed, and very soon the ship was so near, that they could communicate by signs with those on board of her. A boat sent off from her, soon took up the shipwrecked party, and brought them on board; she proved to be an English merchant-vessel, bound for New York. Enfeebled almost to the point of death, they needed, and received careful nursing; and favorable winds soon brought them safely to their "desired haven."

Several years since, Francis and Ferdinand wrote to some friends in Germany, that they were established as merchants in New Orleans, with a moderate competence; but the letter was written in so cheerful a tone, that one might have believed they had found some great treasure there. Any one who is acquainted with their history, however, must know that it was the Spirit of the Lord which had brought them reconciliation, peace and joy, and thus, though they were poor, had made them rich. Of their "brother John," whom they mentioned with cordial affection, they had once received intelligence from China; he had written to them joyfully that the Lord was daily adding to His Church such as should be saved.

* * * * * *

This, my children, is the history of "the Little Apostle"—a story of the Spirit of the Lord. May it add to your pleasure in the Whitsuntide festival! But know this, too; that this is not the first time in this book that we find the Spirit of the Lord; for it was that Spirit which sanctified the Christmas Eve for Anthony and Marietta, that raised the soul of the dying Rudhelm to the cross of

Christ, and taught little Magdalene the cheering Resurrection faith.

Pray, pray for this, above all other gifts, for you must be sure of this truth, which, as the great lesson of this book, may well be its closing words: "No man can call Jesus Christ Lord, except through the Holy Ghost!"

Deacidified using the Bookkeeper process.
Neutralizing agent: Magnesium Oxide
Treatment Date: Oct. 2005

PreservationTechnologies
A WORLD LEADER IN PAPER PRESERVATION

111 Thomson Park Drive
Cranberry Township, PA 16066
(724) 779-2111

LIBRARY OF CONGRESS

0 016 063 975 1

www.ingramcontent.com/pod-product-compliance
Lightning Source LLC
Chambersburg PA
CBHW022139160426
43197CB00009B/1351